Jill's Toad

Written by Rozanne Lanczak Williams
Created by Sue Lewis
Illustrated by Patty Briles

Creative Teaching Press

Jill's Toad
© 2002 Creative Teaching Press, Inc.
Written by Rozanne Lanczak Williams
Illustrated by Patty Briles
Project Manager: Sue Lewis
Project Director: Carolea Williams

Published in the United States of America by:
Creative Teaching Press, Inc.
P.O. Box 2723
Huntington Beach, CA 92647-0723

All rights reserved. No part of this book may be reproduced in any form without the written permission of Creative Teaching Press, Inc.

ISBN: 1-57471-877-0
CTP 3243

Jill's toad can croak, "Hello!"

Jill's toad can play in the snow.

Jill's toad can hop
on the road.

Jill's toad is on the go!

Jill's toad can float
in the boat.

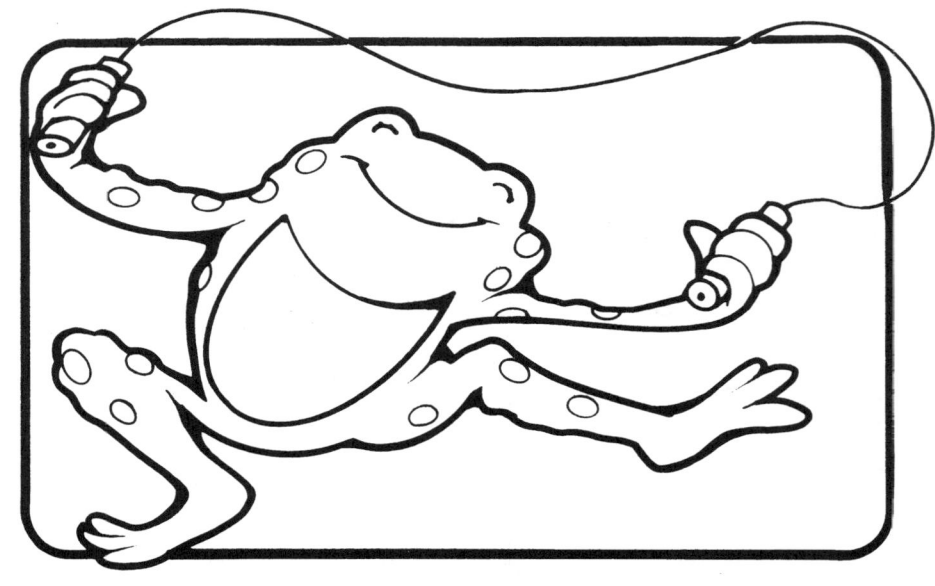

Jill's toad can jump rope.

Jill's toad can write a note.

And Jill's toad can tell a joke!

Create your own book!

Write and illustrate a book about Jill's toad. Write about yourself, too! Make a cover and the inside pages of your story in the shape of a toad.

Words in *Jill's Toad*

Long o	High-Frequency Words	Other
toad	can	Jill's
road	play	jump
croak	in	write
hello	the	tell
go	on	hop
snow	is	ha! ha! ha!
float	a	
boat	and	
rope		
note		
joke		